APPLE FRACTIONS

by Jerry Pallotta
Illustrated by Rob Bolster

Cartwheel
B·O·O·K·S ®
SCHOLASTIC INC.

New York   Toronto   London   Auckland   Sydney   Mexico City   New Delhi   Hong Kong

Thank you to all the kids and teachers at Johnny Appleseed Elementary School in Leominster, Massachusetts.
—— Jerry Pallotta

This book is dedicated to the men and women who live and work in the "Big Apple," New York City.
—— Rob Bolster

Text copyright © 2002 by Jerry Pallotta.
Illustrations copyright © 2002 by Rob Bolster.
All rights reserved. Published by Scholastic Inc.
SCHOLASTIC, CARTWHEEL BOOKS, and associated logos
are trademarks and/or registered trademarks of Scholastic Inc.

Library of Congress Cataloging-in-Publication Data
Pallotta, Jerry.
  Apple fractions / by Jerry Pallotta ; illustrated by Rob Bolster.
     p. cm.
Summary: Describes a variety of apples and uses them to introduce
fractions.
  ISBN 0-439-38901-1 (pbk.)
  1. Fractions--Juvenile literature. 2. Apples--Juvenile literature.
[1. Fractions. 2. Apples.] I. Bolster, Rob, ill. II. Title.
  QA117 .P148 2002
  513.2'6--dc21

                        2002002205

ISBN 978-0-439-38901-3

28 27 26 25   13 14 15 16

Printed in the U.S.A.   08
This edition first printing, October 2002

This book is about apples and math. Apples are a fruit that we eat.
They do not grow under rocks. They do not swim in the ocean.
They are not made in a factory. Apples grow on trees.

APPLES

Thousands of different types of apples are grown around the world. Apples can be red, yellow, green, or some combination of these three colors.

FRACTIONS

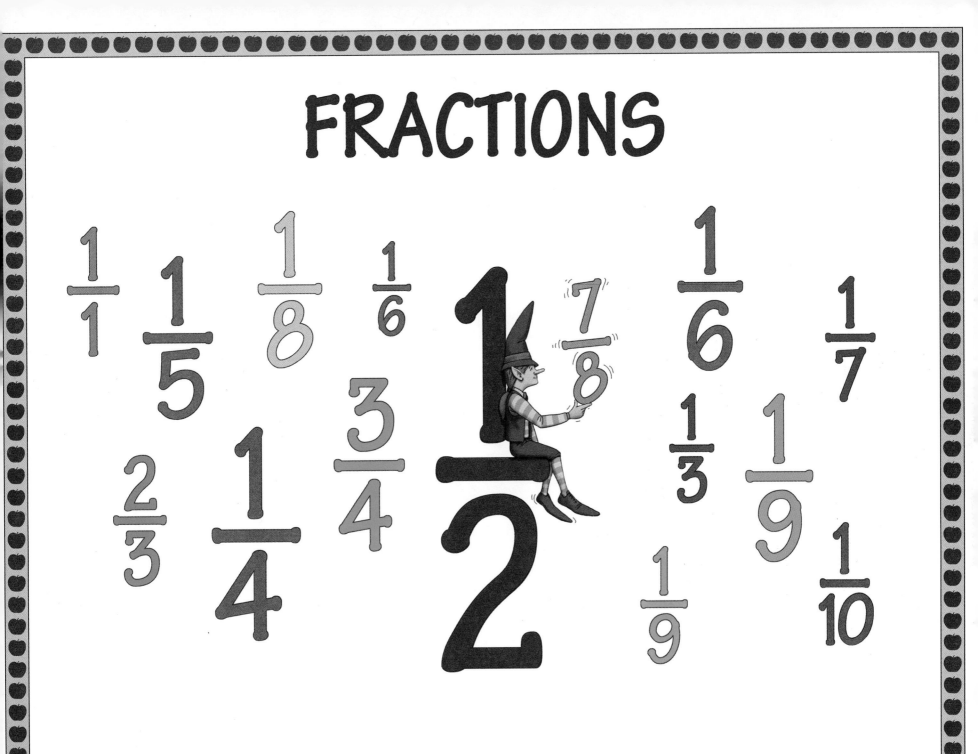

What is a fraction? A fraction is a part of a whole thing. A fraction is shown by placing one number over another number. A line separates the numbers.

McINTOSH

Here is one whole McIntosh apple. This type of apple can be both a drink and a snack. A McIntosh is very juicy, but it is also crunchy and fun to eat.

one whole

If you would like to share one apple with someone, what would you do?
Two kids, one apple? A solution would be to divide the apple into two parts.
A stem for one kid and the apple for the other kid. No, that's not fair!

$\frac{1}{2}$ *one-half*

How about a better way? Divide the apple into two equal parts.
Here is one-half of the apple.

one-half $\frac{1}{2}$

Here is the other half of the apple. Two kids, one apple, two halves.
Sharing apples and learning fractions is fun.

GOLDEN DELICIOUS

This apple is called a Golden Delicious.
On the outside, it has a thin skin. On the inside, the fruit is soft.

three-thirds $\frac{3}{3}$

What if three friends want to eat this apple?
Three friends, one apple, three equal parts.

$\frac{1}{3}$ one-third

Here is one-third of a Golden Delicious apple. Not all apples have white fruit. The inside of this apple is light yellow.

two-thirds $\frac{2}{3}$

$$\frac{1}{3} + \frac{2}{3} = \frac{3}{3}$$

Here is what is left over from one whole apple after taking away one-third.
Two-thirds! One-third plus two-thirds equals three-thirds.
Three-thirds is a whole apple.

GRANNY SMITH

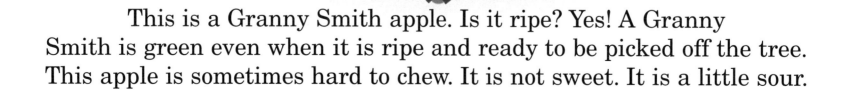

This is a Granny Smith apple. Is it ripe? Yes! A Granny
Smith is green even when it is ripe and ready to be picked off the tree.
This apple is sometimes hard to chew. It is not sweet. It is a little sour.

one whole $\dfrac{1}{1}$

What if four people in a family want to eat one Granny Smith apple?
The apple would need to be divided into four pieces.

Each family member would get one-fourth. The top number of a fraction is called the numerator. The numerator of this fraction is one.

three-fourths $\frac{3}{4}$

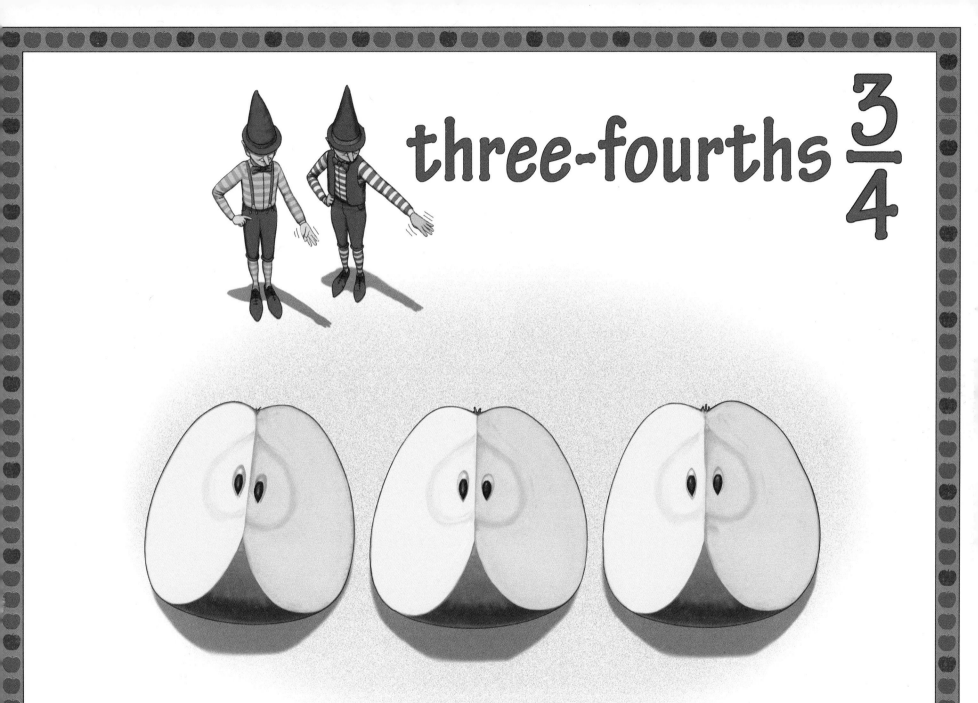

The bottom number of a fraction is called the denominator.
The fraction three-fourths has a numerator of three and a denominator of four.

RED DELICIOUS

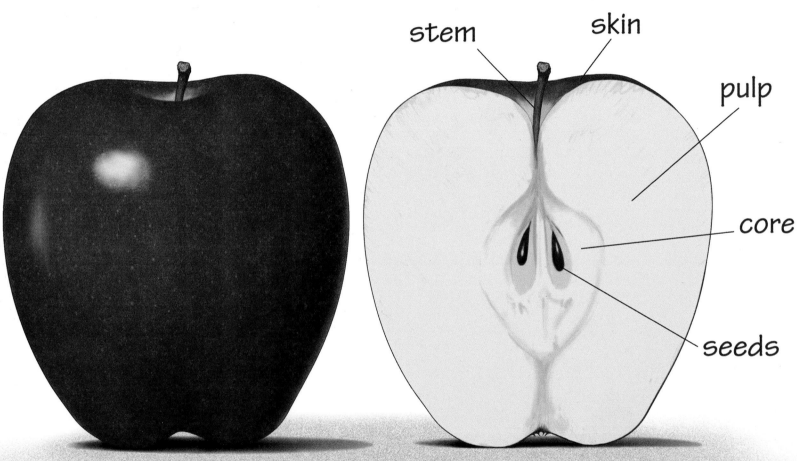

Which apple tastes the best? Everyone has a favorite. Many people think the Red Delicious apple is the best looking and the best tasting.

It is time to learn the parts of an apple: stem, skin, pulp, core, and seeds. Most apples have ten seeds.

ORANGE

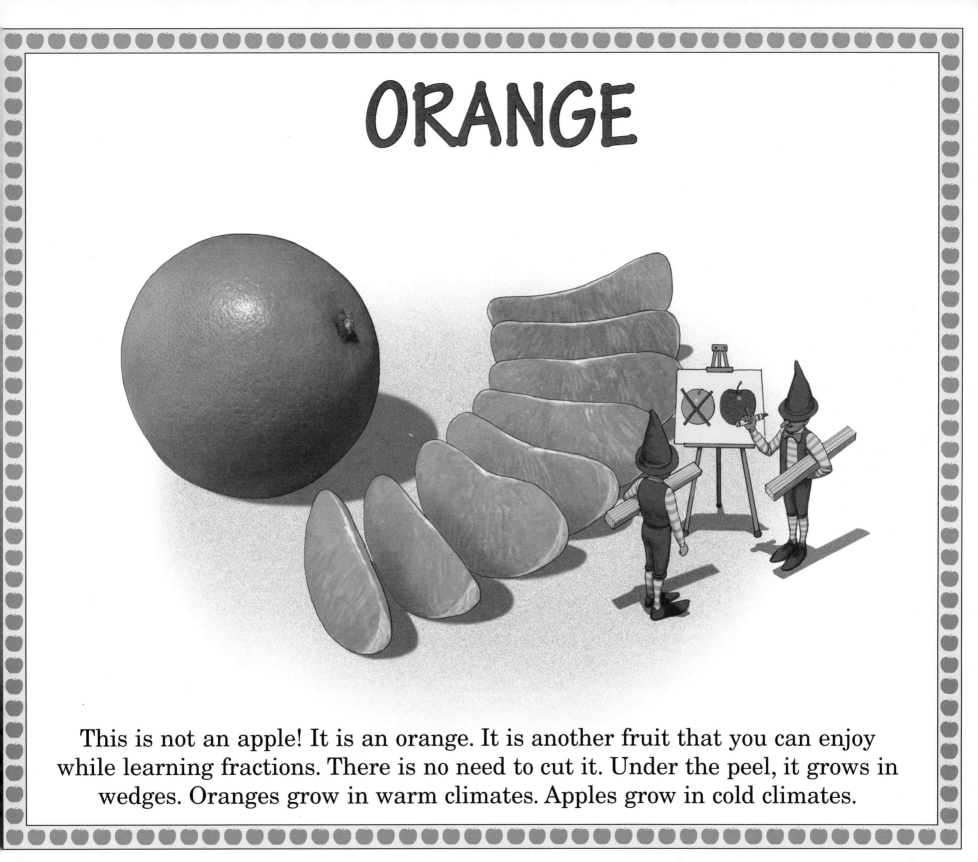

This is not an apple! It is an orange. It is another fruit that you can enjoy while learning fractions. There is no need to cut it. Under the peel, it grows in wedges. Oranges grow in warm climates. Apples grow in cold climates.

$\frac{1}{5}$ one-fifth

GALA

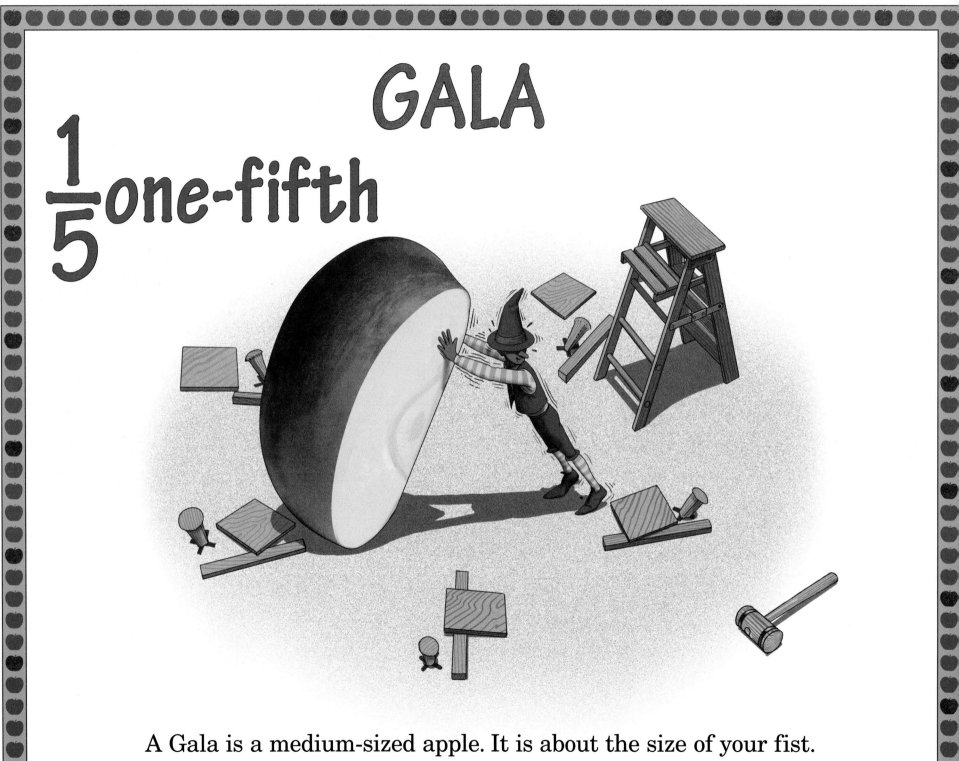

A Gala is a medium-sized apple. It is about the size of your fist.
The largest apples are as big as grapefruits. The smallest are the size of cherries.

four-fifths $\frac{4}{5}$

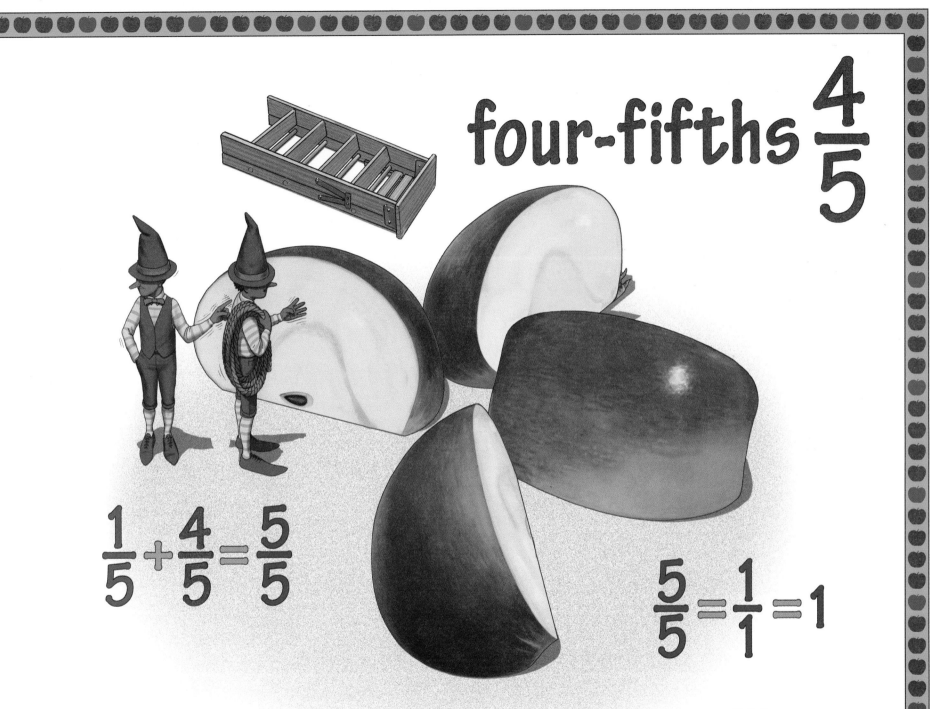

$$\frac{1}{5} + \frac{4}{5} = \frac{5}{5}$$

$$\frac{5}{5} = \frac{1}{1} = 1$$

This Gala is cut into five equal pieces. Each piece is one-fifth.
One-fifth plus four-fifths equals five-fifths. When the numbers above and
below the line are the same, the fraction equals one whole.

$\frac{1}{6}$ **one-sixth**

APPLE BLOSSOM

Apple trees grow flowers in the spring. Bees fly from flower to flower and spread pollen on the apple blossoms. This is the start of an apple. Thank you, bees! Without bees, there would be no apples.

five-sixths $\frac{5}{6}$

BEES

One-sixth of the bees is busy working. Five-sixths of the bees are looking for another apple tree or maybe even a pear tree, a plum tree, or a cherry tree.

CORTLAND

If you cut an apple sideways, you will notice that the core is shaped like a star.
Dividing the apple sideways instead of from top to bottom
will not give you equal parts. The top, the middle, and the bottom
of an apple are each a different width.

$\frac{6}{7}$ six-sevenths

$\frac{1}{7}$ one-seventh

There are three basic types of apples:
"eating apples," "juice apples," and "baking apples." No matter how you slice it,
a Cortland is a wonderful apple to use when baking a pie.

ASIAN PEAR

Sometimes looks can fool you. This fruit looks like an apple.
It is shaped like an apple. But it tastes like a pear. Why? It is a pear!
Let's use this Asian Pear to learn about improper fractions.

$\dfrac{1}{8}$

one-eighth

eight-eighths

$\dfrac{1}{8} + \dfrac{8}{8} = \dfrac{9}{8}$

$\dfrac{8}{8}$

If this pear is divided into eight equal pieces, each piece is one-eighth of the pear.
A whole pear is eight-eighths. Imagine you have nine-eighths. Nine-eighths is an improper fraction. You would have to use two pears to make nine-eighths. Nine-eighths is really one whole pear and one-eighth of a second pear.

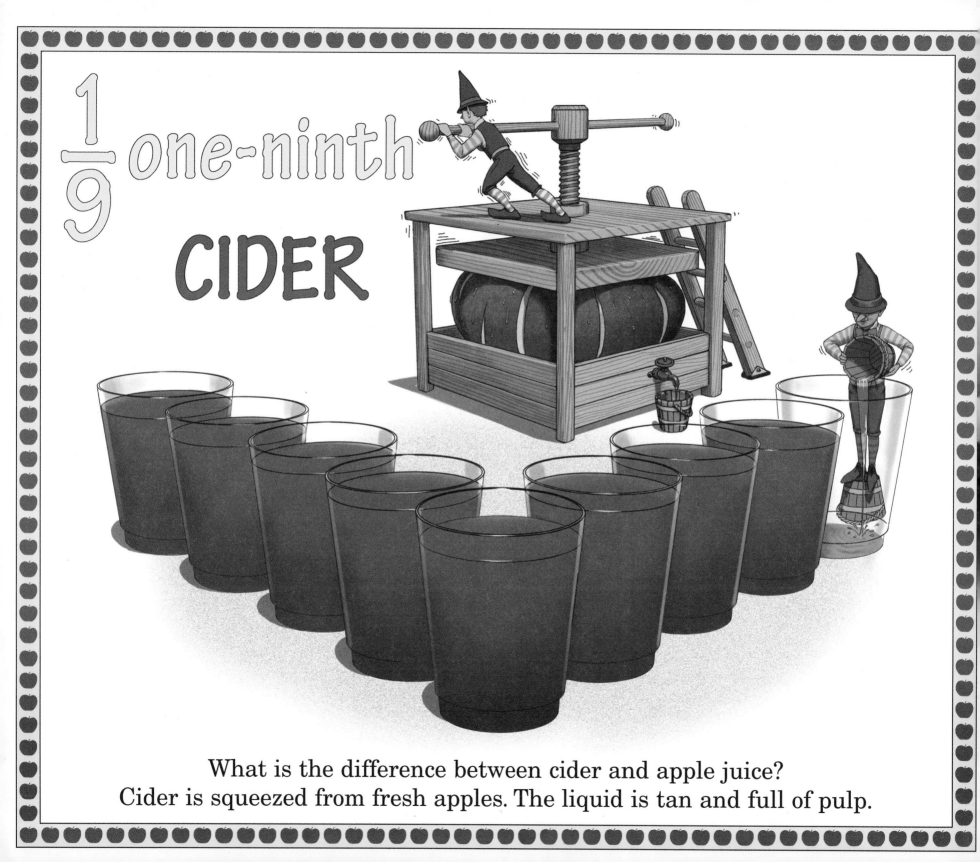

$\frac{1}{9}$ one-ninth
CIDER

What is the difference between cider and apple juice?
Cider is squeezed from fresh apples. The liquid is tan and full of pulp.

APPLE JUICE

Apple juice is cider that has been filtered. The tan pulp is removed and the apple juice is clear. Are you thirsty? Would you like one-fourth, one-half, three-fourths, or one whole glass of apple juice?

$\dfrac{1}{10}$ one-tenth

nine-tenths $\dfrac{9}{10}$

Here are ten apples. Oh, well . . . there were ten apples.
Here are nine apples. One has been eaten. One-tenth is now a core.
Nine-tenths are whole apples.

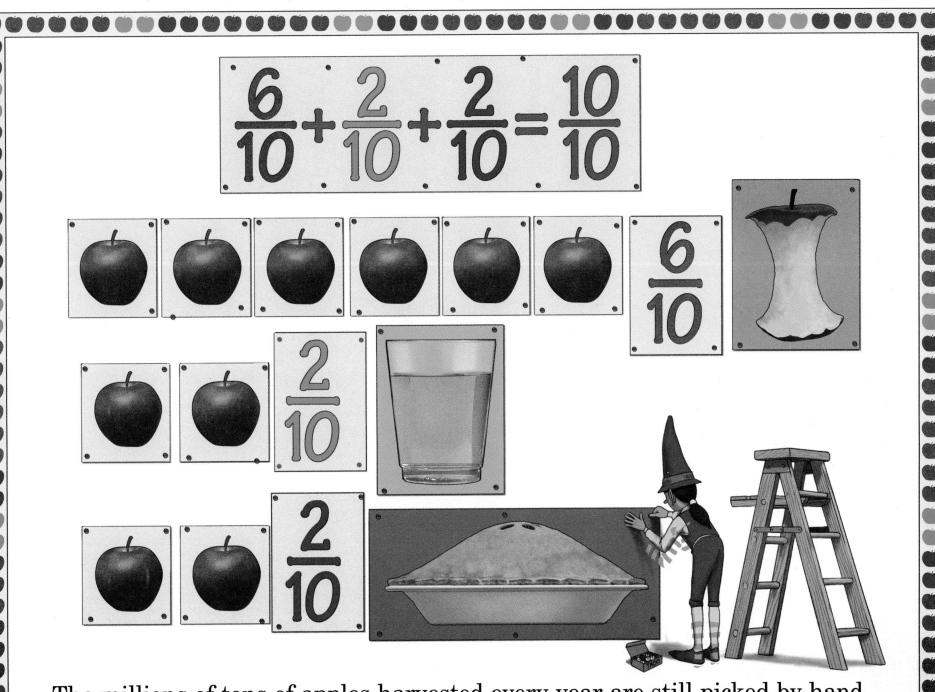

$$\frac{6}{10} + \frac{2}{10} + \frac{2}{10} = \frac{10}{10}$$

$\frac{6}{10}$

$\frac{2}{10}$

$\frac{2}{10}$

The millions of tons of apples harvested every year are still picked by hand. Out of every ten apples, six are eaten fresh. Two out of every ten are squeezed into cider and apple juice. The remaining two out of every ten are made into canned apples, pie filling, jams, jellies, dried apples, and apple butter.

APPLE PIE

While you were reading this book, someone baked an apple pie.
Let's eat a fraction of it!